# Home Décor
# using Grommets

LEISURE ARTS, INC. • Maumelle, Arkansas

## Editorial Staff

**Vice President of Publishing:** Peg Couch
**Editorial Director:** Tona Jolly
**Director of Product Development:**
Lauren Binci
**Technical Editors:** Mary Sullivan Hutcheson,
Lisa Lancaster, and Jean Lewis
**Art Category Manager:** Lora Puls
**Graphic Artist:** Kellie McAnulty
**Photography Technical Manager:**
Stephanie Johnson
**Prepress Technician:** Janie Marie Wright
**Contributing Photographer:** Jason Masters
**Contributing Photo Stylist:** Lori Wenger

## Business Staff

**President and Chief Executive Officer:** Fred F. Pruss
**Vice President of Operations:** Donald Borin
**Vice President of Sales:** Martha Adams
**Chief Financial Officer:** Tiffany P. Childers
**Controller:** Teresa Eby
**Information Technology Manager:** Brian Roden
**Director of E-Commerce:** Mark Hawkins

Library of Congress Control Number: 2017961422
ISBN/EAN: 978-1-4647-7217-7
UPC: 0-28906-07324-9

Who would have thought that simple little rings made of metal or plastic would have revolutionized the home décor world? Since their introduction as a fun and functional way to hang curtains, grommets have started popping up everywhere.

My innovative collection of grommet uses include adding pizzazz to a basic lampshade and an elegant touch to throw pillows. Be sure to check out the Scarf & Purse Keeper and the Phone Charging Pouch if you are looking for quick and easy gift ideas. From a simple pot holder to an oversized Floor Cushion to a soft-sided Catch-All, there's a grommeted project just perfect for you!

# BILLIE STEWARD

Billie Steward enjoys sewing "anything for the home" but says pillows and custom-fit slipcovers are her favorite projects.

"I love making pillows because you can get so creative," she says. "I love a lot of different styles, but French farmhouse has to be my favorite."

A former designer and technical writer for Leisure Arts, Billie says she received her love for design and her ability to create what she sees in her mind from her mother.

"About 17 years ago, I was asked by an interior designer friend if I would make a few pillows for a client of hers. Of course I said yes and that job led to another which then led to my custom slipcover business."

Her designs have appeared in several Arkansas home decorating and lifestyle magazines.

Billie now works full time at a gift shop, teaches dance cardio classes two nights a week, and spends her spare time doting on her four cats or relaxing at nearby Greer's Ferry Lake.

# table of contents

JOY | CALVIN MILLER
KINDNESS | CALVIN MILLER
PEACE | CALVIN MILLER
FAITHFULNESS | CALVIN MILLER
SELF-CONTROL | CALVIN MILLER

# LAMPSHADE

## SHOPPING LIST

- purchased lampshade
- $^3/_8$" wide ribbon - measure around top and bottom of lampshade; add measurements together and add 16"
- eight $^5/_{16}$" diameter metal grommets
- grommet-setting tool
- hammer
- craft knife
- hot glue gun and glue sticks

## Making the Lampshade

*Read pages 60-64 before beginning your project.*

1. Cut ribbon length into eight equal pieces.

2. Follow manufacturer's instructions to attach 4 grommets about 1" below the top edge of the lampshade equal distances apart.

3. Repeat Step 2 to attach remaining grommets about 1" above bottom edge of the lampshade equal distances apart and alternating with top grommets.

4. Place one ribbon end through one grommet; fold and glue end about 1" to inside of lampshade. Pull remaining ribbon end taut and place through adjacent grommet; fold and glue to inside of lampshade. Repeat to glue remaining lengths of ribbon through grommets.

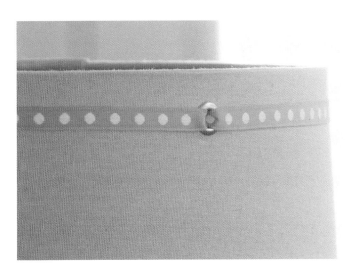

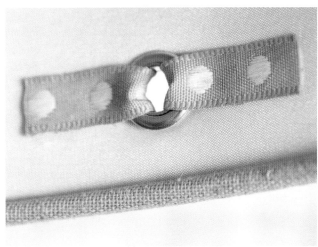

# KITCHEN TOWEL HOLDER

## SHOPPING LIST

○ two $4^1/_2$" x $11^1/_2$" pieces of fabric

○ $4^1/_2$" x $11^1/_2$" piece of Pellon® Craft-Fuse® #808

○ $1^9/_{16}$" diameter plastic grommet

○ $3/_4$" diameter button

## Making the Holder

*Read pages 60-64 before beginning your project. Always match the fabric right sides and raw edges and use a $1/_2$" seam allowance unless otherwise indicated.*

1. Fuse the interfacing to the wrong side of one fabric piece.

2. Leaving an opening for turning, sew the fabric pieces together around the outer edges.

3. Trim the corners. Turn the hanger right side out and press. Topstitch $1/_4$" from the outer edges.

4. Follow the manufacturer's instructions to center and attach the grommet about 1" from one end of the hanger.

5. Center and sew the button about $4^1/_2$" from the opposite end of the hanger.

6. Make a buttonhole for your button about $3/_4$" from button end of hanger. Fold end of hanger over and button in place.

POT
HOLDER

## SHOPPING LIST

*Fabric amounts and instructions given are for making one pot holder.*

- ○ two 8¹/₄" x 10¹/₄" pieces of fabric for pot holder front and back

- ○ 8¹/₄" x 8¹/₂" piece of coordinating fabric for pocket

- ○ 8¹/₄" x 10¹/₄" piece of Insul-Bright™ needled insulated lining

- ○ 8¹/₄" x 10¹/₄" piece of cotton batting

- ○ extra wide double fold bias tape

- ○ ¹⁵/₃₂" diameter metal grommet

- ○ grommet-setting tool

- ○ hammer

- ○ water-soluble fabric marking pen

## Making the Pot Holder

*Read pages 60-64 before beginning your project.*

**1.** On pot holder front, begin $1^1/4$" from one short edge and use marking pen to draw parallel lines 1" apart.

**2.** Stack pieces together in the following order: pot holder back (wrong side up), Insul-Bright, batting, and pot holder front (right side up); pin layers together. Stitch along marked lines through all layers.

**3.** To hem pocket, press one short edge $^1/2$" to wrong side; press $^1/2$" to wrong side again. Topstitch along inner folded edge.

**4.** Place pocket right side up on front; baste around all edges of pot holder. *(**Note:** Batting is closest to pocket and Insul-Bright is closest to heat source.)*

**5.** Cut two $9^1/4$" and two $10^1/4$" pieces of bias tape. Notice that the folded bias tape is wider on one side. This side will be sewn to the back of the pot holder. Unfold one $10^1/4$" piece of tape and align the raw edge with one long side on the back of the pot holder; pin. Stitch along the fold. Refold the bias tape, enclosing the raw edge. Topstitch the bias tape in place. Repeat for the remaining long edge of the pot holder.

**6.** Repeat Step 5 to attach one $9^1/4$" piece of bias tape to the top edge of the pot holder, turning the short raw ends of the tape about $^1/2$" to wrong side. Repeat for the bottom edge of the pot holder.

**7.** Follow the manufacturer's instructions to attach the grommet in one upper corner of the pot holder.

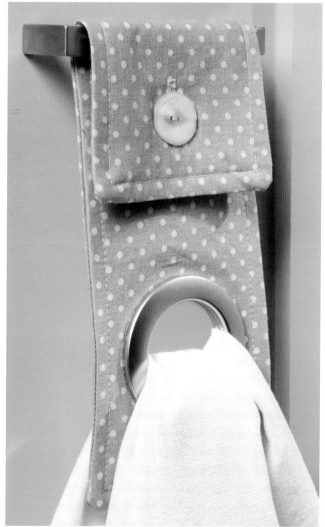

# CURTAINS

## SHOPPING LIST

○ two painter's canvas drop cloths (I used 6 ft x 9 ft drop cloths.)

○ 2" wide ribbon (twice the finished curtain lengths plus 12")

○ 1⁹/₁₆" diameter plastic grommets (I used 6 grommets for each of my 62" wide curtain panels.)

## Making each Curtain Panel

*Read pages 60-64 before beginning your project.*

1. Measure from the top of the curtain rod to the floor. Add 9¹/₂"; this will be the cut length of the curtain panel.

2. Decide how wide the finished panel should be. My panel is 62" wide. Add 8"; this will be the cut width of the curtain panel.

3. Cut a drop cloth panel the measurements determined in Steps 1-2.

4. To hem the sides, press each side edge 2" to the wrong side; press 2" to the wrong side again. Topstitch the hems in place.

5. To hem the top, press the edge ¹/₂" to the wrong side; press 4" to the wrong side again. Topstitch in place.

6. To hem the bottom, press the bottom edge 2" to the wrong side; press 2" to the wrong side again. Topstitch the hem in place.

7. For the ribbon trim, cut a ribbon length 6" longer than the curtain panel. Press each cut edge 1" to the wrong side. Wrapping 2" to the back at the top and bottom, pin the ribbon to the panel along the inside center edge of the panel. Topstitch the ribbon in place, catching the ribbon on the wrong side in the stitching.

8. Starting close to the side hems and evenly spacing the grommets across the panel, follow the manufacturer's instructions to attach 6 grommets to the panel top about 1" below the top edge. My grommets are about 7³/₄" apart.

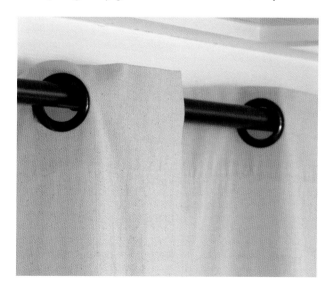

# TABLE RUNNER

## SHOPPING LIST

*Yardage is based on 43"/44" wide fabric with a usable width of 40".*

- ○ 1³/₄ yds of fabric for table runner

- ○ 2 yds of fabric for lining and ruffles

- ○ six 1" diameter plastic grommets

## Cutting the Pieces

**From fabric for table runner:**
- Cut table runner 20" x 54".

**From fabric for lining and ruffles:**
- Cut 2 ruffles 5" wide across the width of the fabric.
- Cut lining 20" x 54".

## Making the Table Runner

*Read pages 60-64 before beginning your project. Always match the fabric right sides and raw edges and use a $1/2$" seam allowance unless otherwise indicated.*

1. Matching right sides, fold one ruffle in half; sew along each short edge (**Fig. 1**). Clip corners and turn ruffle right side out; press. Repeat with remaining ruffle.

2. Baste raw edges of ruffle together $3/8$" from raw edges. Baste again $1/4$" from raw edges. Repeat with remaining ruffle.

3. Pull top basting threads to gather ruffles to about 18" wide. Baste 1 ruffle to each end of runner, leaving $5/8$" on each side (**Fig. 2**).

4. Leaving an opening for turning and with ruffles sandwiched in between, sew the runner and lining together around the outer edges.

5. Clip the corners. Turn the runner right side out and press. Slipstitch opening closed.

6. Follow the manufacturer's instructions to attach three grommets about 4" apart and 2" from top of ruffle on each end of table runner.

**Fig. 1**

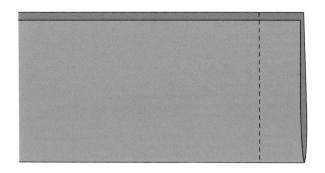

**Fig. 2**

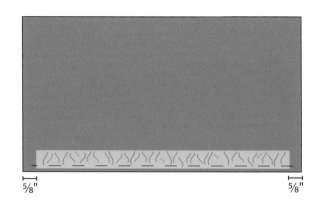

5/8"          5/8"

# NESTED
# BASKETS

## SHOPPING LIST

○  1$^3$/$_4$ yds of 36" wide charcoal felt

○  1$^3$/$_4$ yds of 36" wide blue felt

○  2 packages of Pellon® Fuse-N-Shape™ medium weight two-sided fusible interfacing

○  six 1$^9$/$_{16}$" diameter plastic grommets

## Cutting the Pieces

### Large Basket

**From each color of felt:**
- Cut two $13^1/_4$" x $5^3/_4$" long sides.
- Cut two $9^3/_4$" x $5^3/_4$" short ends.
- Cut one $13^1/_4$" x $9^3/_4$" bottom.

**From interfacing:**
- Cut two 12" x $4^1/_2$" long sides.
- Cut one 12" x $8^1/_2$" bottom.

### Medium Basket

**From each color of felt:**
- Cut two $12^1/_4$" x $5^1/_4$" long sides.
- Cut two $8^3/_4$" x $5^1/_4$" short ends.
- Cut one $12^1/_4$" x $8^3/_4$" bottom.

**From interfacing:**
- Cut two 11" x 4" long sides.
- Cut one 11" x $7^1/_2$" bottom.

### Small Basket

**From each color of felt:**
- Cut two $10^3/_4$" x $5^1/_4$" long sides.
- Cut two $7^1/_4$" x $5^1/_4$" short ends.
- Cut one $10^3/_4$" x $7^1/_4$" bottom.

**From interfacing:**
- Cut two $9^1/_2$" x 4" long sides.
- Cut one $9^1/_2$" x 6" bottom.

## Making Each Basket

*Read pages 60-64 before beginning your project.*

*Always use a $5/_8$" seam allowance when sewing. Backstitch at the beginning and ending of your stitching to lock the stitches in place.*

1. Center the interfacing bottom on the charcoal felt bottom. Matching the outer edges, place the blue felt bottom over the interfacing. Follow the manufacturer's instructions to fuse the interfacing to the felt bottoms. Repeat to fuse the interfacing between the felt long sides.

2. Starting and stopping $5/_8$" from the edges, sew the long sides and short ends together, forming a rectangle. Starting and stopping $5/_8$" from the edges, topstitch along one edge of each long side and short end; these will be the top edges.

3. Starting and stopping $5/_8$" from the edges, sew the bottom to the sides and ends.

4. Follow the manufacturer's instructions to center and attach a grommet about $3/_4$" from the top edge on each short end.

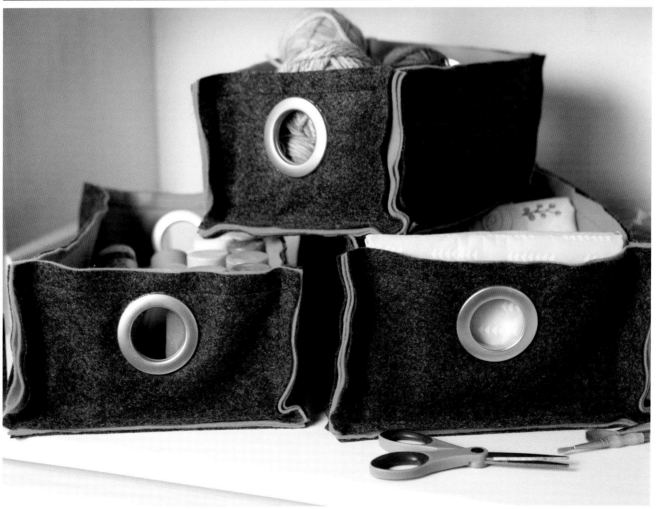

# TISSUE BOX COVER

## SHOPPING LIST

- $17^{1}/_{2}$" square of fabric
- $17^{1}/_{2}$" square of Pellon® Craft-Fuse® interfacing
- $1^{9}/_{16}$" diameter plastic grommet
- water -soluble fabric marking pen

## Making the Tissue Box Cover

*Read pages 60-64 before beginning your project. Always match the fabric right sides and raw edges and use a ¹/₂" seam allowance unless otherwise indicated.*

1. Follow the manufacturer's instructions to fuse the interfacing to the wrong side of the fabric.

2. Referring to **Fig. 1**, draw cutting lines on the interfacing side of the fabric. Cut along the drawn lines. Discard the 6" squares.

3. Matching adjacent edges, sew the sides together, creating a box.

4. To hem the bottom raw edges, press the fabric ¹/₂" to the wrong side; press ¹/₂" to the wrong side again. Topstitch the hem in place.

5. Follow the manufacturer's instructions to center and attach the grommet to the tissue box cover top.

**Fig. 1**

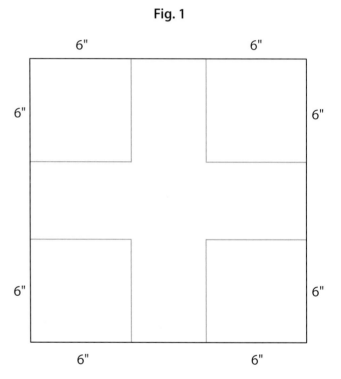

# LUMBAR PILLOW

My pillow was actually made from one fabric. I used the wrong side of the fabric for the front and back of the pillow and the right side of the fabric for the contrasting pillow overlay. Often the wrong side of the fabric can create just the look you need for a very interesting pillow!

## SHOPPING LIST

*Yardage is based on 43"/44" wide fabric with a usable width of 40".*

- ○ ½ yd of fabric for pillow front and back

- ○ ⅜ yd of fabric for contrasting pillow overlay

- ○ three 1" diameter plastic grommets

- ○ 12" x 16" pillow form

- ○ 14" zipper

## Cutting the Pieces

**From fabric for pillow:**
- Cut pillow front 13" x 17".
- Cut upper pillow back 12" x 17".
- Cut lower pillow back 2" x 17".

**From fabric for contrasting pillow overlay:**
- Cut contrasting pillow overlay 8" x 17".

## Making the Pillow

*Read pages 60-64 before beginning your project. Always match the fabric right sides and raw edges and use a $1/2$" seam allowance unless otherwise indicated.*

1. To hem contrasting pillow overlay, press one long edge $1/2$" to wrong side; press $1/2$" to wrong side again. Topstitch along inner folded edge.

2. Follow the manufacturer's instructions to attach three grommets about $2^5/8$" apart and $7/8$" from the hemmed edge of the contrasting pillow overlay.

3. Matching wrong side of contrasting pillow overlay to right side of pillow front, baste along raw edges.

4. To make pillow back, use a long basting stitch to sew upper and lower pillow back along one long edge. Press seam allowances open. Centering seamline over zipper teeth, pin. Topstitch $1/4$" from each edge of seamline, catching zipper tape in stitching.

5. Sew pillow front to pillow back. Trim the corners. Turn the pillow right side out and press. Remove basting stitches to expose zipper. Insert pillow form.

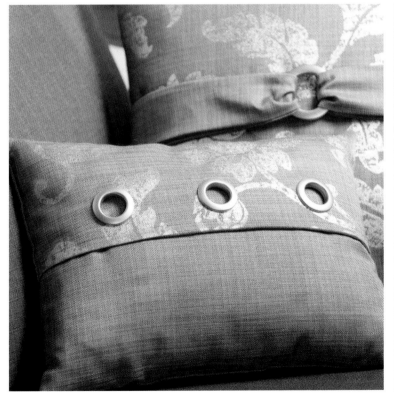

# SQUARE PILLOW

My pillow was actually made from one fabric. I used the right side of the fabric for the pillow and the wrong side of the fabric for the sash. Always look at the wrong side of the fabric; it may present all kinds of possibilities!

## SHOPPING LIST

*Yardage is based on 43"/44" wide fabric with a usable width of 40".*

- ○  ³/₄ yd of fabric for pillow
- ○  ¹/₄ yd of fabric for sash
- ○  1⁹/₁₆" diameter plastic grommet
- ○  20" x 20" pillow form
- ○  18" zipper

## Cutting the Pieces

**From fabric for pillow:**
- Cut pillow front 20" x 20".
- Cut upper pillow back 19" x 20".
- Cut lower pillow back 2" x 20".

**From fabric for sash:**
- Cut 2 sash strips 3" x 40".

## Making the Pillow

*Read pages 60-64 before beginning your project. Always match the fabric right sides and raw edges and use a ¹/₂" seam allowance unless otherwise indicated.*

**1.** Sew sash strips together along each long edge; turn right side out.

**2.** To make 2 sashes, cut sash strip in half. Snap grommet together. Place one end of each sash through the grommet. Centering grommet and pulling sashes taut, baste raw ends of each sash to opposite sides of pillow front. Trim ends of sashes even with pillow front as needed. Set pillow front aside.

**3.** To make pillow back, use a long basting stitch to sew upper and lower pillow backs together along one long edge. Press seam allowances open. Centering seamline over zipper teeth, pin. Topstitch ¹/₄" from each edge of seamline, catching zipper tape in stitching.

**4.** Sew pillow front to pillow back. Trim the corners. Turn the pillow right side out and press. Remove basting stitches to expose zipper. Insert pillow form.

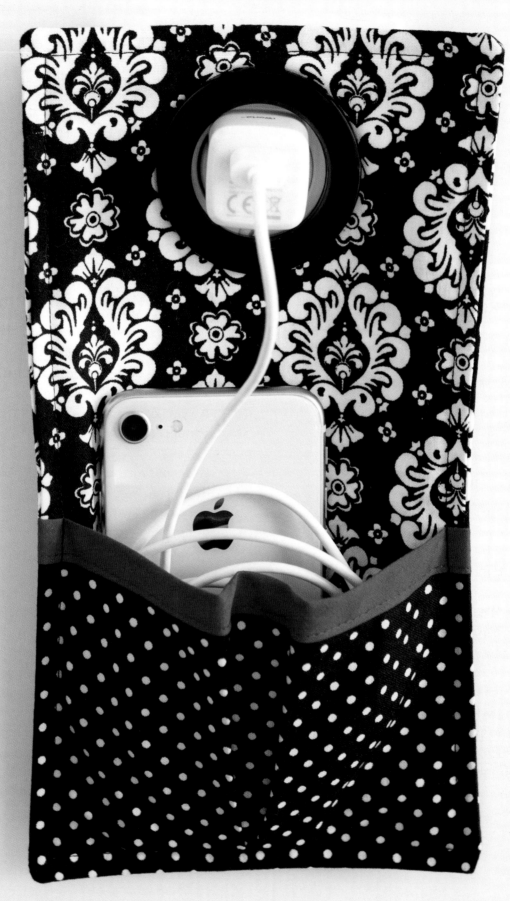

# PHONE CHARGING POUCH

## SHOPPING LIST

- two 6½" x 11" pieces of fabric for base
- 8" x 4¾" piece of fabric for pocket
- 7½" length of extra wide double fold bias tape
- 6½" x 11" piece of nonwoven fusible stabilizer such as Pellon® Craft-Fuse®
- 1⁹⁄₁₆" diameter plastic grommet

## Making the Pouch

*Read pages 60-64 before beginning your project. Always match the fabric right sides and raw edges and use a ½" seam allowance unless otherwise indicated.*

1. Notice that the folded bias tape is wider on one side. This side will be sewn to the back of the pocket. To finish the pocket top edge, unfold the wider edge of the tape and align the raw edge with one long edge of the pocket; pin and stitch along the fold. Refold the bias tape, enclosing the raw edge. Topstitch the tape in place, being sure to catch the tape on the wrong side.

2. Matching the lower edges, pin the pocket right side up on the right side of one base piece on the side edges (you will have excess fabric in the pocket for the center pleat). Baste the side edges to the base. Fold and press the pleat flat on the pocket front; be sure the folds meet at the bottom center. Baste in place.

3. Follow the manufacturer's instructions to fuse the interfacing to the wrong side of the remaining base piece. Leaving a 4" opening for turning, sew the base pieces together around the outer edges.

4. Trim the corners. Turn the pouch right side out and press. Slipstitch the opening closed. Topstitch ¼" from the outer edges.

5. Follow the manufacturer's instructions to center and attach the grommet about ½" from the pouch top edge.

**Finished Width:** My shade is 34" wide but could easily be adjusted for a window as wide as 39".

FAUX
ROMAN
SHADE

## SHOPPING LIST

*Yardage is based on 43"/44" wide fabric with a usable width of 40".*

○  1¼ yds of fabric for shade

○  1⅜ yds of fabric for lining and ties

○  spring tension rod

○  two 1" diameter plastic grommets

## Cutting the Pieces

**From fabric for shade:**
- Cut shade 35" x 38" (**OR** desired finished width +1" x 38".)

**From fabric for lining:**
- Cut lining same size as shade.
- Cut 2 ties $2^1/_2$" x $46^1/_2$", pieced if needed.

## Making the Shade

*Read pages 60-64 before beginning your project. Always match the fabric right sides and raw edges and use a $^1/_2$" seam allowance unless otherwise indicated.*

1. Leaving an opening for turning, sew shade and lining together. Clip corners and turn shade right side out; press. Slipstitch opening closed.

2. To make rod casing, fold top edge 3" to lining side of shade. Topstitch along edge.

3. Follow the manufacturer's instructions to attach one grommet about $5^1/_2$" from side and $3^1/_2$" from top on each upper corner of shade.

4. For each tie, press each raw edge $^1/_4$" to wrong side. Match wrong sides and press tie in half. Topstitch along edges of tie.

5. Place rod through casing and insert in window. Place 1 tie through each grommet. Fold lower edge of shade in about 4" folds until shade is desired length. Tie the ends in bows to hold folds in place.

# RIBBON BOXES

## SHOPPING LIST ────────────

- ○ $7^5/_8$" x 11" x $4^1/_4$" photo storage box

- ○ three 45mm screw together oval metal grommets
  **OR** five $5/_{16}$" diameter and three $15/_{32}$" diameter metal grommets

- ○ grommet setting tool(s); refer to grommet packages

- ○ hammer

- ○ craft knife

- ○ cardstock in color to match dividers (included with photo box) and craft glue – optional, if you want to divide the box interior (see page 43)

- ○ 11" length of $1/_4$" diameter dowel, two $5/_{16}$" diameter grommets, large ball head push pin, and hot glue gun with glue sticks – optional, if you want a rod to keep ribbon spools in place.

## Making the Box

1. Plan where you would like the grommets on one long side of the photo box, being sure to allow room for the box lid. I centered my grommets both vertically and horizontally on the box side. Mark the center for each grommet.

2. Follow the manufacturer's instructions to attach the grommets to the box, using the craft knife for cutting.

3. For a box with inside dividers, first decide how many dividers you would like. To attach each divider, cut four 1½" squares of cardstock. Fold the squares in half. Glue half of a folded square at each end of the divider, aligning the fold with the divider bottom edge. Glue the remaining two folded squares in the same position on the other side of the divider. Allow the glue to dry. Place the dividers in the box as desired. Glue the folded squares to the box.

4. For a box with a ribbon rod, attach a grommet to the center of one short side of the photo box. Hot glue the barrel of the remaining grommet to the opposite side of the box, on the INSIDE of the box (**Fig. 2**). Insert the push pin into one dowel end. Thread the dowel through the grommeted hole in the box, through the ribbon spools, and rest the dowel end in the glued-on grommet.

**Fig. 2**

**Finished size:** 21" diameter x 11" high

# CATCH-ALL

## SHOPPING LIST

*Yardage is based on 43"/44" wide fabric with a usable width of 40".*

- ○ 2 yds green fabric
- ○ 2 yds blue fabric
- ○ 5 yds of Pellon® Craft-Fuse® interfacing
- ○ four 1" diameter plastic grommets
- ○ 22" square of 1/4" thick foam core board
- ○ two 30" lengths of thick nylon rope
- ○ clear tape
- ○ fabric glue
- ○ water-soluble fabric marking pen
- ○ paper to make circle pattern

## Cutting the Pieces

### From each color of fabric:
- Cut one $15^1/_2$" x 67" side.
- Cut one 21" diameter bottom (see **Cutting a Circle**, page 64).

### From green fabric:
- Cut one 22" diameter bottom.

### From interfacing:
- Cut two $15^1/_2$" x 67" sides.
- Cut two 20" diameter bottoms.

### From foam core board:
- Cut one 20" diameter inner bottom (use paper to make a circle pattern).

## Making the Catch-All

*Read pages 60-64 before beginning your project. Always match the fabric right sides and raw edges and use a $^1/_2$" seam allowance unless otherwise indicated.*

1. Follow the manufacturer's instructions to fuse the interfacing side to the wrong side of each fabric side. Center and fuse the interfacing bottoms to the 21" diameter fabric bottoms.

2. Sew the short ends of a fabric side together, forming a ring; press the seam allowances open. Repeat with remaining fabric side.

3. Sew the rings together along one long edge.

4. Turn the ring right side out and press, aligning the long edges. Topstitch $^1/_4$" from the folded edge. This is the top edge. Baste the bottom edges together $^3/_8$" from the outer edge.

5. Matching the wrong sides, baste the fabric 21" diameter bottoms together $^3/_8$" from the outer edge.

6. Matching the outer fabrics, sew the side to the 21" diameter bottom, easing any excess fabric as necessary.

7. Fold the top edge over about $3^1/_2$" and press. Follow the manufacturer's instructions to attach the grommets to the side about $3^1/_2$" apart, placing them on opposite sides of the catch-all, and centering them on the folded area.

8. For each rope handle, tie a knot close to one end of one piece of rope. Thread the rope through a grommet, from back to front, and then back through the adjacent grommet, from front to back. Tie a knot close to the end. Place tape around rope near each knot. Trim the excess rope, cutting through the tape.

9. Center the foam core board circle on the wrong side of the 22" diameter fabric bottom. Wrap the fabric the the wrong side of the foam core board circle and glue in place. Place the covered circle in the catch-all.

# FLOOR CUSHION

## SHOPPING LIST ——————————

*Yardage is based on 43"/44" wide fabric with a usable width of 40".*

- ○ 2³/₈ yds of black and white striped fabric

- ○ 30" x 52" piece of polyester batting

- ○ 22" x 22" x 4" foam pad

- ○ 5¹/₂ yds of ¹/₄" diameter cotton filler cord for welting

- ○ 27" slipcover or upholstery metal zipper

- ○ four 1" diameter plastic grommets

## Cutting the Pieces

**From black and white striped fabric:**
- Cut 1 *lengthwise* boxing strip 5" x 74".
- Cut 1 *lengthwise* strip 3" x 66". Cut this strip into 2 zipper boxing strips 3" x 33".
- Cut 1 cushion top and 1 cushion bottom 23" x 23" each.
- Cut 1 welting square 20" x 20".
- Cut 2 grommet hole backings 5" x 10".
- Cut 2 handles 3" x 13".

## Making the Floor Cushion

*Read pages 60-64 before beginning your project.*
*Always match the fabric right sides and raw edges and use*
*a $1/2$" seam allowance unless otherwise indicated.*

**1.** Centering one edge of the foam pad on one short edge of the batting, wrap the batting around the foam pad. Carefully pulling the batting taut, whipstitch the raw edges of the batting together at the foam pad edge.

**2.** On one remaining side of the foam pad, trim the batting away along the top edge. Do not trim the batting at the short sides. Fold the batting in at the short sides. Fold the long edge of the batting over the foam pad and whipstitch the batting together at the edge. Repeat for the remaining side.

**3.** Use the welting square and follow **Making Welting**, page 61, to make $5^1/_2$ yds of $1^3/_4$" wide welting.

**4.** Follow **Attaching Welting**, page 63, to attach welting to cushion top and bottom.

**5.** To make zipper boxing, use a long basting stitch to sew the zipper boxing strips together along one long edge. Press seam allowances open. Centering zipper boxing seamline over zipper teeth, pin. Topstitch $1/4$" from each edge of seamline, catching zipper tape in stitching.

**6.** Matching center of zipper boxing to center of one side of cushion top and allowing zipper boxing to extend around corners, sew zipper boxing to cushion top. To make turning corners easier, clip seam allowance of sides at cushion top corners. Side of cushion with zipper is the back of the cushion.

**7.** Press each short edge of boxing strip 4" to wrong side. Matching center of boxing strip to side opposite zipper boxing, and allowing boxing strip to extend around corners, sew boxing strip to cushion top. Clip corners in same manner as previous. Folded ends of boxing strip will cover ends of zipper.

**8.** Following manufacturer's instructions, attach two grommets to boxing strip on two opposite sides of cushion. Mine are centered on the sides and placed about 3" apart.

**9.** Matching right side of one grommet hole backing to wrong side of boxing strip, center grommet hole backing under grommets. Sew along previous stitching line. Repeat with remaining grommet hole backing under grommets on opposite side.

**10.** Catching grommet hole backings in seam, sew zipper boxing and boxing strip to cushion bottom. Clip corners in same manner as previous.

**11.** Press each long edge of one handle $1/2$" to wrong side. Matching pressed edges, press handle in half. Topstitch $1/4$" from each long edge. Repeat for remaining handle.

**12.** Insert one handle end through grommets and overlap ends $3/4$". Sew ends together. Pull handle through grommets so overlap is behind boxing strip. Repeat with remaining handle.

**13.** Remove basting stitches to expose zipper. Insert batting-covered foam pad in cushion.

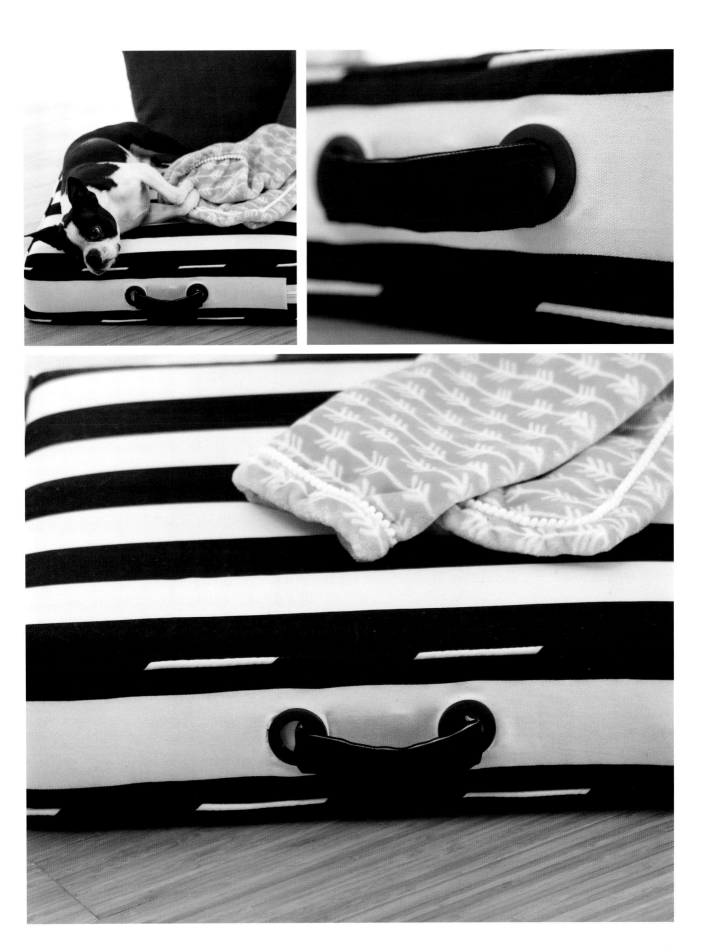

# SCARF & PURSE KEEPER

## SHOPPING LIST ————————————

*Yardage is based on 43"/44" wide fabric with a usable width of 40".*

○ $1/2$ yd of natural-colored cotton duck

○ $3/4$ yd of $5/8$" wide black grosgrain ribbon

○ $1/2$ yd of sew-in hook and loop fastener

○ three $1^9/_{16}$" diameter plastic grommets

○ two $5/_{32}$" diameter metal grommets

○ grommet-setting tool

○ hammer

○ fabric glue

## Cutting the Pieces

### From cotton duck:
- Cut 1 keeper front and 1 keeper back 7" x 25".
- Cut 2 purse holders 7" x 7".

### From ribbon:
- Cut 4 ribbon lengths $6^{1}/_{2}$" long.

## Making the Keeper

*Read pages 60-64 before beginning your project. Always match the fabric right sides and raw edges and use a $^{1}/_{2}$" seam allowance unless otherwise indicated.*

**1.** Leaving an opening for turning, sew the keeper front and back together around the outer edges.

**2.** Trim the corners. Turn the keeper right side out and press. Slipstitch opening closed.

**3.** Turning raw edges to wrong side even with sides of keeper, glue 1 ribbon length along bottom edge of keeper. Glue additional ribbon lengths $5^{1}/_{2}$", 10", and $14^{1}/_{2}$" from the top edge of the keeper.

**4.** Follow the manufacturer's instructions to attach the metal grommets in each top corner about $^{1}/_{2}$" from the top edge of the keeper.

**5.** Follow the manufacturer's instructions to center and attach the plastic grommets in each upper section of the keeper.

**6.** To make one purse holder, press all sides $^{1}/_{2}$" to wrong side. Fold square in half and topstitch approximately $^{1}/_{8}$" from all sides. Sew hook side of fastener to one end of holder and loop side of fastener to opposite end of holder. Repeat with remaining purse holder and hook and loop fastener.

**7.** Stitching around hook side of fastener, sew purse holders about $8^{1}/_{4}$" and 4" from bottom of keeper.

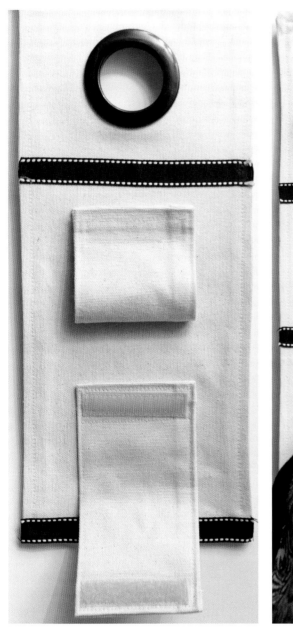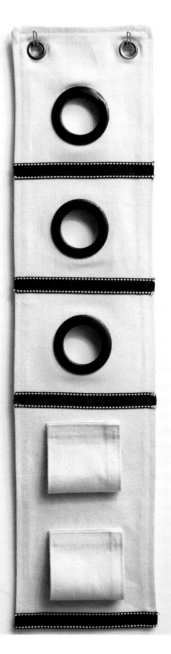

# STEP STOOL
# SEAT COVER

## SHOPPING LIST

*Yardage is based on 43"/44" wide fabric with a usable width of 40".*

- ○ floral fabric (see Steps 1-2)
- ○ $^3/_4$ yd of ticking stripe fabric for welting and pleats
- ○ $^1/_4$" diameter cotton filler cord for welting (enough to go completely around the stool top plus 5")
- ○ eight $^{15}/_{32}$" diameter metal grommets
- ○ grommet setting tool; refer to grommet package
- ○ hammer
- ○ paper for pattern

# Making the Step Stool Cover

*Read pages 60-64 before beginning your project. Always match the fabric right sides and raw edges and use a $1/2$" seam allowance unless otherwise indicated.*

**1.** To make a pattern, turn the stool upside down onto the paper. Draw around the stool top. Add $1/2$" seam allowance to all sides and cut out. Fold the pattern in half and in half again. Mark the corner centers. Use the pattern to cut the cover top, clipping the fabric at the corner marks.

**2.** For the skirt, cut two $7^1/2$" floral fabric pieces each the length of two opposite sides plus 5". Cut two $7^1/2$" floral fabric pieces each the length of the remaining two opposite sides plus 5".

**3.** For the skirt pleat inserts, cut four 5" x $7^1/2$" ticking stripe fabric pieces.

**4.** For the welting, cut an 18" square of ticking stripe fabric. Cutting a 2" wide continuous bias strip, follow **Making Welting**, page 61, to make welting; trim the bias strip 2" longer than the cord. Set aside the remaining bias strip for the grommet ties.

**5.** Follow **Attaching Welting,** page 63, to attach welting to the cover top.

**6.** Referring to **Fig. 1**, sew the pleat inserts and skirt pieces together. Sew the remaining free ends together to make a fabric loop.

**7.** For the bottom hem, press one long edge $1/2$" to the wrong side; press $1/2$" to the wrong side again. Topstitch the hem in place.

**8.** To make the corner pleats, measure out 2" at the top and bottom edges on either side on one pleat insert seam and place a mark on the skirt fabric (**Fig. 2**).

**9.** Matching the wrong sides, fold and press the skirt fabric at the marks to crease the pleats.

**10.** Bring the folded edges to the center of the insert. The pleats should meet and cover the insert (**Fig.3**); baste.

Fig. 1

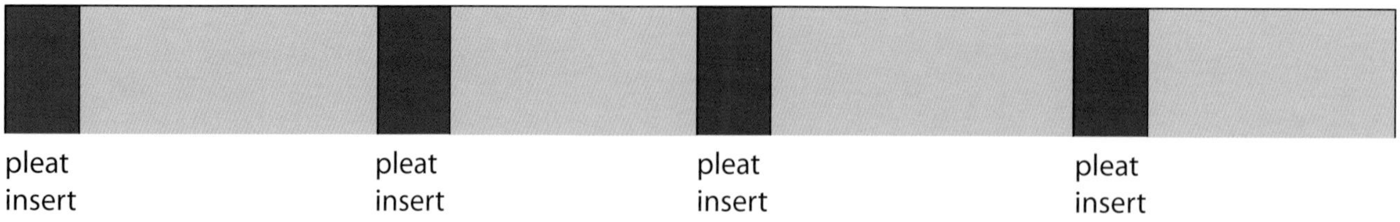

pleat insert   pleat insert   pleat insert   pleat insert

**11.** With the pleats centered on each corner, baste the skirt to the top through all layers.

**12.** Turn the cover right side out. Follow the manufacturer's instructions to attach a grommet to each side of each pleat.

**13.** For the grommet ties, cut a 2" x 56" bias ticking stripe fabric strip. Fold the strip in half lengthwise and press. Fold each raw edge to the center crease and press. Topstitch along the fold, closing the open edges.

**14.** Cut the ticking stripe strip into 4 equal lengths. Tie a length through each set of grommets.

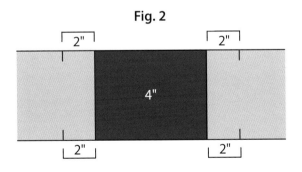

**Fig. 2**

2"

2"

4"

2"

2"

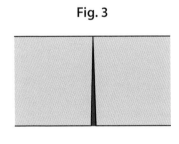

**Fig. 3**

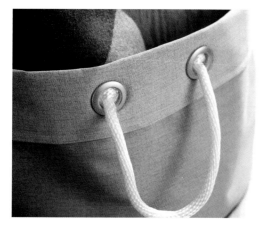

# GENERAL INSTRUCTIONS

## SELECTING FABRICS

The type of fabric you choose should depend on how the project will be used and where it will be placed in your home. My projects were made from lightweight cotton fabric, heavy cotton duck, and home decorating fabric. Check labels on fabric bolts for care instructions. Allow extra fabric for one-way designs or large patterns.

## PREPARING FABRICS

If your project will require washing or dry cleaning, wash or dry clean your fabric before cutting out pieces. This will preshrink the fabric and remove any excess dye. But be aware that washing some fabrics may dull the shiny finish.

Knowing the basics of fabric grain is essential to cutting fabric pieces correctly; cutting fabric pieces on grain eliminates stretching and puckering of the finished project. Grain refers to the direction of threads woven in the fabric. Crosswise grain refers to the threads running the width of the fabric from selvage to selvage. Lengthwise grain refers to the threads running the length of the fabric, parallel to the selvages. Bias refers to the diagonal direction on a piece of fabric in relation to crosswise and lengthwise grain (**Fig. 1**).

Before cutting out pieces, it is important that the cut edges of your fabric are straight or "squared." Matching right sides and selvages, fold fabric in half; press. Refer to **Fig. 2** and place a square ruler or carpenter's square on fabric, with one edge aligned with selvages and an adjacent edge close to bottom of fabric. Mark a straight line along bottom edge of ruler; move ruler and continue line to fold. Cut fabric along drawn line.

For pattern fabrics with designs that are printed slightly off-grain, the finished project will look better if you square the fabric along the pattern design instead of the crosswise grain. Lay fabric flat. Using one edge of a square ruler or carpenter's square, draw a line across bottom edge of fabric from selvage to selvage, following the pattern rather than the grain. Cut fabric along drawn line.

Individual project instructions indicate size to cut fabric pieces. Start from squared edge when measuring and cutting pieces.

## Making Welting

1.  Using fabric square indicated in project instructions, cut square in half diagonally to make 2 triangles.

2.  With right sides together and using a $1/4$" seam allowance, sew triangles together (**Fig. 3**); press seam allowances open.

3.  On wrong side of fabric, draw lines the width of the binding as specified in the project instructions (**Fig. 4**). Cut off any remaining fabric less than this width.

**Fig. 1**

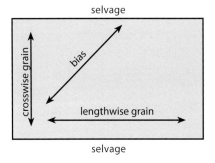

**Fig. 2**

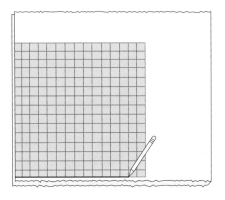

**Fig. 3**

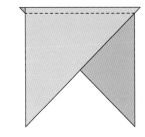

**Fig. 4**

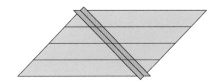

4. With right sides inside, bring short edges together to form a tube; match raw edges so that first drawn line of top section meets second drawn line of bottom section (**Fig. 5**).

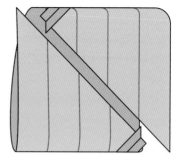

**Fig. 5**

5. Carefully pin edges together by inserting pins through drawn lines at the point where drawn lines intersect, making sure the pins go through intersections on both sides. Using a $1/4$" seam allowance, sew edges together. Press seam allowances open.

6. To cut a continuous strip, begin cutting along first drawn line (**Fig. 6**). Continue cutting along drawn line around tube.

**Fig. 6**

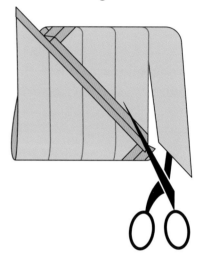

7. Trim ends of bias strip square.

8. Lay cord along center of bias strip on wrong side of fabric; fold strip over cord. Using a zipper foot, machine baste along length of strip close to cord (**Fig. 7**). Trim seam allowances to $1/2$" wide.

**Fig. 7**

## Attaching Welting

1. Matching raw edges and beginning and ending 3" from ends of welting, baste welting to right side of fabric. To make turning corners easier, clip seam allowances of welting at corners.

2. Remove approximately 3" of seam at one end of welting; fold fabric away from cord. Trim remaining end of welting so that cord ends meet exactly (**Fig. 8**).

3. Fold short edge of welting fabric $\frac{1}{2}$" to wrong side; fold fabric back over area where ends meet (**Fig. 9**).

4. Baste remainder of welting to fabric close to cord (**Fig. 10**).

**Fig. 8**

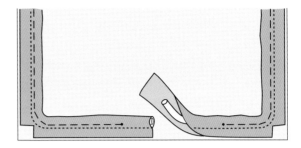

**Fig. 9**

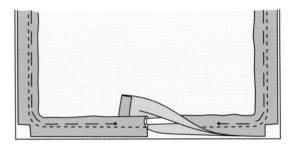

**Fig. 10**

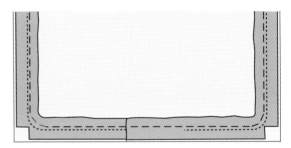

## Cutting a Circle

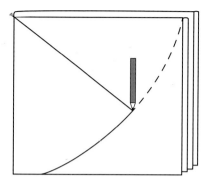

1. Divide the circle measurement given in the project instructions in half.

2. Referring to the **Cutting Diagram**, tie one end of a string to a pen (for making paper patterns) or a fabric marking pen (for marking directly on fabric). Insert a thumbtack through the string at the measurement from the pen determined in Step 1.

3. Fold the paper or fabric in half from top to bottom and again from left to right. Insert the thumbtack through the corner of the paper or fabric as shown; draw the cutting line.

4. Cut along the drawn line through all layers. Unfold the paper or fabric.